The Rule(s) of Our Game(s)

Larry Miller

ROG, Inc.

ISBN 978-0-578-07430-6

*I dedicate this book to my beautiful wife Cathy
and our precious three daughters
Taylor, Mackenzie and Shelby*

CONTENTS

INTRODUCTION

We live in a world filled with chaos.

Nothing seems the same after 9/11.

We are at war with one another.

Hatred abounds.

Terror reins.

People are dying.

We finally seem to have come to a consensus that global warming is a reality, yet we don't have a comprehensive plan in place to address it.

We know the destruction of rain forests will have a dramatic affect on the environment, but little is being done to stop to it.

We can barely bring ourselves to talk about sex, yet sex crimes are at an all time high.

What kind of mess are we leaving for our children and their children to clean up?

Is this the way it is going to be? Is this the way it has to be?

How did we end up in this situation?

Is there anything we can do to change it?

Is time running out? Have we made so many mistakes along the way that it's hopeless?

Are we even living our lives correctly? Maybe we have it all wrong. What if we have it backward? Maybe life on earth as we know it is not reality, but an illusion. If it is an illusion, is it like a game? If so, are we playing it correctly? If there are rules, wouldn't it help to know what they are so we can play the game better?

THE GAME

Assume for a moment that before you were born you had a say in the kind of life you were going to experience—you had some influence in planning the circumstances that you would be born into. No matter what happened after you were born, you knew that you would return to a safe, warm and wonderful place that would accept you back as you were unconditionally. Would you behave differently as you went through life? Would you get as stressed out when "bad" things happen that you have no control over? If you lost your job and couldn't pay the rent, would you feel better if you knew in the end it wouldn't matter? Would it help to know that the pain is temporary and will not last for eternity?

If those were truly the rules and you could do anything you wanted on earth, it would really open things up. You could raise hell if you wanted to. No curfew, no accountability and no worries. No catches.

The Catch

There is a catch, of course. You are accountable for your actions. Accountability always has been and always will be there. That is why we find ourselves in the situation we are in. Not only is there accountability for actions, but also for every action there is a corresponding reaction. That is just how it works—and the sooner it's understood the better.

We live on a wonderful planet that has finite space and resources. For millions of years it seemed so big it appeared almost infinite in its size and all that it had to offer. However, today the world's population has reached numbers that are almost incomprehensible.

We are starting to recognize that there are people next to us. In fact there are lots of people next to us. We are bumping into each other in the grocery store, in movie lines and on freeways. We have to wait in line just about everywhere we go. Some people have started to ask what affect this is having on our unlimited resources. Maybe, just maybe, they are not as unlimited as we once thought.

Limited Resources

Our natural resources are limited and will not last forever at our current consumption rates. Although this book does not provide detailed statistics on when they will expire, considerable documentation available from other sources supports the premise that they will expire at some point in the near future.

If, in fact, this is a game we are playing and there are consequences for all of your actions, you need to understand what the rules are and the natural consequences of your actions. Then you'll be better equipped to figure out what you should be doing to get yourself out of the situation you're in.

RULE #2
Freedom of Choice

We will come back to Rule #1.

Have you ever wondered why "bad" things happen to good people and "good" things happen to bad people? Why is someone else always lucky? Why do some people seem to have everything?

Even deeper, have you ever wondered about your purpose in life? What are you doing here on this earth? Do you have any control over your life or are you just subject to whatever comes your way? Do you feel empowered or helpless? It is natural for most people at some point in their life to ask these types of questions. Most people don't actually get real answers, though.

Rule #2 is the greatest gift to human kind: *Freedom of Choice. Freedom of Choice* is a wonderful thing. Unfortunately, in our world there are still many countries where it is not allowed. *Freedom of Choice* is a fundamental right given to all of us whether or not the government recognizes it. The problem with *Freedom of Choice* is that with every choice, there is a natural consequence. The consequence could be viewed as a good thing or a bad thing, but there will always be a "thing." In today's society we often do not make the connection between the choices we make and their natural consequences.

A Reaction for Every Action

A little girl is riding her bike, pulls out on a busy street and is killed by a passing car. It is a horrible tragedy for all involved including the car driver, and the girl and her family. When the girl set out that day to ride her bike, it was not her choice to die. She did not intend to get hit by a car. The accident was a natural consequence of her choice to ride out into the street. For every action, there is a reaction. There is no getting around it. Bad things can happen to good people.

When people do not see the connection between their choices and the consequences, there is no accountability. Whatever happens to them is someone else's fault. They are victims. They convince themselves that they had no control over the situation, but they couldn't be more wrong. People who do this are doomed to blindly flounder in the consequences of their own actions indefinitely.

It's important for you to understand this rule. It is foundational and can change your life if you embrace it.

You Make Choices Every Day

If you wake up one day and find yourself in a situation you do not like, one where you are unhappy, choose differently. It is that simple. We tell ourselves over and over again that we have no control over the situation that we are in. We tell ourselves so many times that we believe it. It is simply not true. If you do not like your situation, change it. Take control. Take responsibility. Don't blame other people—do something to change it!

Will it change instantly? That depends on what it is that you are trying to change and how long it took you to get where you are. If it took you 15 years to rack up over $100,000 in credit card debt, the debt will not go away overnight. But you can start to chip away at it one dollar at a time and over time that debt will go away.

Baby Steps

Start paying for items in cash. A shirt that requires two $20 bills from your wallet looks a lot different than a little tiny paper receipt. Start asking yourself if it's really what you want when you are about to purchase something. Is it helping you toward your goal of getting debt free? Only go to the grocery store when you are not hungry and when you have a list. Take some time to write out a budget and go back at the end of the month to see how you did. For every dollar you save, put half of it toward paying down the principal and put half in a savings account. Start saving $100 dollars a month and then after some of your debt starts to shrink make it $200 a month and so on. None of these are earth-shattering changes but cumulatively over time they will make an enormous difference in your financial situation.

If you are 50 pounds overweight, that weight will not come off overnight because it didn't show up overnight. Instead of trying the latest and greatest fad diet that you know will fail, make a commitment to change slowly over time. Start exercising on a regular basis and slowly reduce your food portions. But don't over do it right away or you will set yourself up for failure. It took time to get into the eating habits you have today and it will take time to change them—but they can be changed.

Walk three days a week for 30 minutes and focus on food portion control. Do this for a month and all of a sudden you have created a new habit. Begin to add weights once a week and increase your walks to 45 minutes. Do that for another month and you will have changed your habits again. After 100 days you will be well on your way to being a happier, healthier and slimmer person. Take baby steps. Chip away one pound at a time. The changes won't happen overnight, but by gradually increasing exercise and eating right you will start to become who you are and not what you do. That is very powerful.

Many people don't want to take baby steps because they are not "sexy." We live in a society that demands instant gratification. If we can't get it fast we don't want it. We value the immediate.

But the truth is, if you do not like where you are, all you have to do is choose differently.

Make a Plan, Set Goals and Put it in Writing

Come up with small action steps that will gradually get you to where you want to go. Then review where you are on a regular basis.

If you did this in all areas of your life, imagine where you could be in six months, a year, five years or ten years. It would be a much different place than where you are today.

Take responsibility for your life and quit blaming other people. If you use Rule #2 so that it works *for* you and not *against* you, you will live a much happier life.

RULE #3
Laws of the Universe

We live in a very complicated world. There are many things that we do not understand.

Things happen for reasons you may not yet be aware of. Unless you make an attempt to understand how things work, you are subjecting yourself to just going through the motions blindly, triggering events in your life that you had no idea you had any influence on whatsoever.

The universe operates under very distinct rules. These are called *Laws of the Universe*, also known as *Laws of Attraction*. They work as follows: Whatever you send out into the universe comes back. This is true whether you choose to acknowledge it or not.

Your life is an exact mirror of what you have chosen. There is no other way around it. This is how the natural *Laws of the Universe* work. You get what you ask for. Don't believe it? It's true. If you don't like what you see in the mirror, refer back to Rule #2 and choose differently.

Four Simple Steps

Most likely you are not aware of how much power you possess to affect your life and the lives of others. Many people go through life thinking there is some mysterious plan that they are supposed to follow, which will somehow be revealed to them. The reality is that they have had control over their own destiny from the beginning and didn't know it.

The frightening part is how much damage you can do in your life and not be aware of the fact that you have been the one responsible for the damage. Become more aware of your powers. Begin to incorporate these steps in your everyday life. Work on mastering these new skills and be amazed at the changes in your life.

It all starts with simple thought. How are your thoughts having an impact on your life? Thought is a form of energy that has an impact on the universe. It ultimately comes back and has an impact on your life. Throughout the course of a lifetime, the cumulative impact of all your thoughts, both good and bad, is enormous.

If you constantly go through your day having negative thoughts, these thoughts go out into the universe in waves of energy and bounce back to you magnified. The returning negative thoughts are manifested by negative events in your life. It is like you are walking around with a loaded gun firing negative bullets that will eventually find their way back into your life. Is this something you would choose to do if you were aware of the consequences?

Understand the power at your disposal and start using it to your advantage. Consciously make an effort to minimize those negative bullets and start focusing on positive bullets. Watch with wonder and amazement how your life will change for the better.

If you want to increase your influence on your world, follow your positive thoughts by writing them down. Think them first and then write them down. This is why goal writing is so effective. Write down your dreams and desires. This process reinforces your thoughts and amplifies the energy you are sending out into the universe—energy that will come back to you!

Want even more power and influence over your life? Back up your thoughts and written word with action. Take small action steps that reinforce your goals and dreams, and help make them a reality.

Before you entered this world, your soul sat down with God to rough in an outline of what you wanted to experience in this life. They set goals on what to work on in the new upcoming life on earth. Your soul did this in partnership with God. Did your soul want to experience fame or fortune? Did it want to understand pain? Did it have any consequences to pay back from poor choices in previous lives? Did it want to be a mountain climber or a sea diver? Did it want to be black, white or brown? Did it want to play music or sports? Did it want to experience what it is like to be blind or disabled? Did it want to be gay?

This plan was roughed in before you were born with the understanding that only your soul would remember the goals, whatever they were when you came to life. After that, *Laws of the Universe* would start to have an effect.

There is no guarantee that you will accomplish any of the goals your soul set out to do in this lifetime. Depending on what choices you make in life and whether or not you are listening to the yearnings of your soul, you may or may not tackle the life plan that you made in advance. But one thing is for sure; do not wait for this plan to be revealed to you.

Listen to your soul and become an active participant in your life. You have the power to determine your experience in this life; you do not need to sit passively on the sideline waiting for it to unfold. Something will unfold, but will it be what your true desires are? Will it be what you set out to accomplish in the beginning?

There is a point in the movie "Forrest Gump" where Forrest is contemplating life and wonders out loud if you have a destiny in life that will happen no matter what you do, or if you are in total control over what happens to you. He concludes that maybe there is a "little bit of both" going on. There *is* a little bit of both going on. You had a plan in place before you came to this life, your soul was an active participant in formulating that plan. However, it may not happen if you don't start listening to your soul, thinking those positive thoughts, writing down your dreams and desires, and setting and completing action steps to accomplish your goals.

If you have been sitting on the sidelines of life waiting for your destiny to be revealed, become more involved with your life. Start taking some initiative and become a more active partner in your own experience. Then watch the "little bit of both" unfold in your life.

The final step is to have faith. Faith in your destiny. Faith in your part of controlling your life. Faith in your new active partnership with God. Faith in the *Laws of the Universe*. Faith that no matter what happens in this life that you will go back "home" and be loved only to start planning your goals for your next life. This is the cycle of life. This is how our souls try to obtain the mastery that Jesus had. Jesus was a master soul. A master soul is a soul that has completely mastered the *Laws of the Universe*. They know how the laws work and are therefore able to create amazing things, things we call miracles. Jesus knew how the *Laws of the Universe* worked, for this is how he accomplished his miracles. We could all perform miracles if we worked toward the mastery that he had.

So, Rule #2 gives you freedom of choice, but Rule #3 tells you how to choose. Follow these steps to master the *Laws of the Universe*.

1. *Thought*
2. *Word*
3. *Action*
4. *Faith*

That's it, just four simple steps. If you follow them on a regular basis, you will get what you ask for. The universe has no other choice but to give it to you. The real scary part is that people go through their lives on a day-to-day basis blindly putting these powerful tools in motion and they don't even realize what they are doing. They don't understand how dangerous some of their actions are or what the natural consequences will be.

If you understand these concepts and embrace them, your life will change forever (for good or bad, you choose!).

Value Judgments

Before we get into the details of how this process works, let's take a moment to discuss the concepts of good or bad and right or wrong. The universe does not make a judgment call as to whether an action is good or bad, but people do. We do it all the time. We are champions at judging other people. We love it.

Deciding what is right and what is wrong is a value judgment. That is all it is.

The most important thing to understand about value judgments is that they are constantly changing. In Roman times, killing Christians was the right thing to do. Before the Civil War, it was right to own slaves. It used to be right to discriminate against people because of their color or their beliefs. Something is only "right" because someone *said* it is.

As society evolves, so do our value systems. We are constantly revising and changing our beliefs, for good or bad. Be careful the next time you starting judging someone else because of what you think is right or wrong. What you think may not be "in" tomorrow. What you believe will likely change over time. Making judgments on other people based upon a changing set of values is a waste of time and energy. You have better things to do with your time and energy.

What You Think is What You Get

Many successful people know the secret to their own success. They spend their precious time and energy focused on what they want out of life. To truly get what you want, you must follow Rule #3 consistently.

Thought is energy that starts everything. It's very powerful. As humans we are really energy when you break us down at the atomic level. We began our time on this earth as energy and we will end our time here as energy.

The energy of thought is the key to make all things happen. It is the beginning to everything we have, everything we own and everything that is yet to come.

Putting it in Writing is Important

When you focus and think about something you are actually sending energy waves into the universe. The universe receives those thoughts, *materializes* them and sends them back to you.

If you follow your thoughts by putting them in writing, the response you get back is much stronger than if you did not put it in writing. If you follow your thoughts with writing *and action*, the response you get back is exponentially stronger than the response you would have received with just putting it in writing.

Actions, One Baby Step at a Time

If you consistently use thought followed by writing followed by action, you will begin to move mountains. Miracles will occur. Your life will never be the same.

That is why it is so important to put your goals in writing. Every year, every month, every day, put your goals in writing and create small baby action steps that will lead you to your goal. Then, actually take the baby steps and your dreams will come true. It is that easy.

Will it happen over night? No. Will it take effort? Yes. Will you go from being $100,000 in debt to a millionaire by Friday? No. Will you lose your 50 pounds of excess weight before dinner? No. Can you go from being massively in debt to being wealthy? Yes. Can you go from being dangerously overweight to being healthy? Yes. What does it take? Regularly applying thoughts, words and actions to Rules #2 and #3.

If you do this over time there is nothing you cannot accomplish!

No Negatives

Now that you are aware of *Laws of the Universe*, the first thing you need to do is make sure you are not allowing them to work against you. This game of life is hard enough without competing against yourself.

Eliminate all the negative thoughts you have. There is no need for them and they are so corrosive. Stop talking negatively about other people. Nothing good will come of it. Stop physically and emotionally hurting people. You truly are also hurting yourself.

Add good stuff to your life. Put so much good stuff in that there is no room for the bad stuff. Ask yourself how good you feel after listening to three hours of talk radio where all they did was bash other people. You have just immersed yourself in negativity for three hours of your day. What kind of impact do you think that will have on the rest of your day or on the people you interact with? Get rid of the negative stuff, there is no need for it. Listen to music that makes you feel good. Go to the library and check out an audio book and listen to that instead.

If you make a habit of consistently striving to put good stuff in your life, there is no way Rule #3 can work against you. You will start to see progress on your life goals, you will start to feel positive momentum and feel ready for the day instead of being burned out and depressed.

You choose.

The Echo of Life
Author Unknown

A son and his father were walking on the mountains.

Suddenly, the son falls, hurts himself and screams: "AAAhhhhhhhhhh!!!"

To his surprise, he hears the voice repeating, somewhere in the mountain: "AAAhhhhhhhhhh!!!"

Curious, he yells: "Who are you?"

He receives the answer: "Who are you?"

Angered at the response, he screams: "Coward!"

He receives the answer: "Coward!"

He looks to his father and asks: "What's going on?

The father smiles and says: "My son, pay attention."

And then he screams to the mountain: "I admire you!"

The voice answers: "I admire you!"

Again the man screams: "You are a champion!"

The voice answers: "You are a champion!"

The boy is surprised, but does not understand.

Then the father explains: "People call this ECHO, but really this is LIFE.

It gives you back everything you say or do.

Our life is simply a reflection of our actions.

If you want more love in the world, create more love in your heart.

If you want more competence in your team, improve your competence.

This relationship applies to everything, in all aspects of life;

Life will give you back everything you have given to it.

YOUR LIFE IS NOT A COINCIDENCE,
IT'S A REFLECTION OF YOU!

RULE #4
The Bible is Incomplete and Misleading

What does this mean? It means there are many good things in the Bible, but it is not complete. In some instances it is misleading, and this has had an enormous affect on our society for nearly two millennium. And not all of it has been good.

Most people who know the Bible and read it are not aware of the history of how it truly came about. Yet over years, decades and centuries of reading it, it has been assumed that it must be true and accurate. In reality, so much of what we know as fact in life, in truth is not fact at all. Stories passed from lips to lips, from village to village, can become grossly distorted if not completely wrong. In many cases it becomes a well meant reflection on how events and people were perceived by those with their own bias. History is written, and sometimes rewritten, by the winners. It always has been so and it always will be.

Does this mean that everything in the Bible is false testimony? Heavens no. There are many great lessons in the Bible that flow from the fountain of truth. However, there are also misleading testimonies, prejudices and entire missing books that you need to be aware of. After all, if countries are prepared to go to war over religious beliefs, which they have for centuries, perhaps we should take some time to make sure we understand what is based on truth and what is not. That requires discernment.

To start your own evaluation, it is always best to start in the beginning.

In The Beginning

Up to about 3,500 BC, most societies near the Middle East were matrilineal. This means they were ruled by women and everything flowed from women. All power, positions and property were passed through the mother and female kinship. Famous gods who were worshiped during this time were Isis (God-Mother, the Divine One, the Queen of all Gods), Inanna (Goddess of Love, Fertility and War) and Aphrodite (Goddess of Love, Beauty and Sexual Rapture). Women ruled the world!

Sometime after 3500 BC the Indo-Aryan invasion took place, which brought about the concept of supreme male deity, male god with unlimited power. This gradually replaced the worship of the beautiful goddess to strong and masculine gods. The paradigm shifted from female power and dominance to the male. Men ruled the world!

Two Books: One Old and One New

The Bible has been around in various forms for centuries and is broken down into two main books, the Old Testament and the New Testament. The Old Testament is the result of gradual growth over the centuries and deals with the time period before the birth of Jesus Christ. The New Testament picks up at the birth of Jesus Christ, outlines his life story, including his miracles and philosophies on life and also covers his death. We will focus primarily on the New Testament.

Looking for a Messiah

As prophesized in the Old Testament, the Palestinian people were looking for and expecting a messiah to save them from Roman oppression. Messiah literally means one who is anticipated as, regarded as, or professes to be a savior or liberator. Jesus seemed to fit the bill. Many Jews accepted Jesus as the promised messiah from the line of David. Christ literally means messiah.

Jesus was born and the calendar soon changed from BC to AD. The New Testament has many stories relating to the birth of Jesus and some about his childhood until he was about 12, but has relatively little about his life after that until the last three years before he died about the age of 33.

New Testament Written and Rewritten

At that point in history it was customary to pass on stories verbally, but it was very uncommon for them to be written down. Until the birth of Christ, the Bible consisted of the Old Testament. It wasn't until about AD 70, about 40 years after the death of Christ, that the first books of the New Testament began to be written. This was the beginning of Christianity and its separation from Jewish beliefs. This split is ironic in itself, because Jesus was a Jew.

The Gospel of Mark was the first Gospel of the New Testament to be written. It is interesting that Mark was not an apostle, but a follower, as was Luke. Mathew and John were apostles, but their books were written sometime after Mark's. It is argued that Paul, who never met Jesus, had influence over the four Gospels and actually wrote most of the balance of the New Testament. Most of these works were being completed by the end of the second century and were rewritten by nearly the end of the fourth century.

Orthodox vs. Gnostic

After the death of Christ there was a struggle between two religious groups, the Orthodox Christians and the Gnostic Christians.

The Gnostic's believed that Jesus was a spiritual guide on earth and his resurrection was to symbolize how Christ's presence could be experienced in the present. What mattered was not the literal seeing, but the spiritual vision. Gnosis is the Greek word for knowledge. Gnostics believed that to know oneself is to know God, that you could become equal with Jesus, a spiritual master, and with God. Gnostics also believed that you could have direct access to God.

The Orthodox Christians believed in the literal resurrection, that Jesus is Lord Divine and Son of God. He remained forever distinct from the rest of humanity and you could never be on the same level of Jesus or God. The Orthodox believed that God was only accessible to humanity through the Church. Over time the Church organized into a three-rank hierarchy of bishops, priests and deacons who came to believe themselves to be the guardians of the only "True Faith."

Orthodox Christians said that any belief outside of theirs was heresy. Heresy by definition is any doctrine not in line with the official statement of the "faith," not whether or not it is in line with the truth.

They launched an organized campaign to purge all writings and beliefs that did not fall in line with the official statement of the church. This campaign continued over several hundred years from about the time the Gospel of Mark was written until the Council of Nicaea (AD 325) when the Church voted that Jesus was the "only begotten son of the Father." This became the Orthodox creed of the empire and no other variations were tolerated.

Compromises

In the 4th Century, almost 350 years after the death of Christ, the Emperor Theodosius declared Christianity the official religion of the Roman Empire. As Christianity was starting to gain momentum and the number of Christians in Rome was growing, Emperor Constantine the Great, viewed them as support in his struggle to keep the imperial throne from his rival and brother-in-law.

During this period, Constantine escalated the penalty of heresy to death. At the same time, however, two large groups of sun worshipers became prominent. One was devoted to Sol Invictus (the Invincible Sun) and celebrated changes on earth such as the winter solstice. The other sun-worshiping cult popular in Rome at the time was Mithraism. They promoted a belief in the immortality of the soul, Judgment Day and the resurrection of the dead.

Constantine saw a perfect opportunity to blend all three religions together, achieving the political and religious unity he saw as being vital to his own success. Conveniently, Sol Invictus, Mithraism and Christianity were similar enough in several respects to become one.

It is not uncommon for rising religions to blend new traditions with some of the old traditions from the religion being superseded. For example, many of the existing holidays are retained, as well as the worship dates and sacred locations. In addition, many of the same symbols are used. This process helps people adjust to the new religion and is called transmutation. Christianity is a product of transmutation.

For the merge of religions to be successful, a few things needed to be tweaked to make everything fit. It is believed that Jesus was actually born in the springtime, but they moved the celebration of his birth to December 25 so they could celebrate it closer to the winter solstice. Easter is a pagan celebration of the spring solstice, Esthre, so they lined that up with the death and resurrection of Christ. The resurrection of the dead, immortality of the soul and Judgment Day which were part of the Mithraism religion were all blended into the new religion, Christianity.

Christian canonization is taken from the ancient "God-Making" rite of Euhemerus, and the practice of Holy Communion, or "God-Eating," was borrowed from the Aztecs. The concept of Christ dying for our sins is also not new. The Quetzalcoate believed that the self-sacrifice of a young man absolved the sins of his people.

These are but a few examples of how Christianity blended itself with existing beliefs to get to where it is today.

Once the merge was underway, they launched a major smear campaign to discredit the remaining pagan symbols that were not incorporated into the new religion. The pitch fork was a positive symbol in paganism that represented successful fall harvests. It was turned into the devil's pitch fork. The Pentacle, the main pagan symbol for nature worship, became the sign of the devil. The wise horn became the witches' hat. The smear campaign was a success and the myths of evil were born.

Demonizing the Sacred Feminine

With so many pagan symbols being discredited, Constantine and his successors also demonized the pagan belief in the sacred feminine and obliterated the goddess from modern religions.

There is evidence that one of Jesus' messages was that we are all equal in the eyes of God —we are all God's children. This includes all genders and races. Although it is not stated directly, there are also clues that Jesus was married to Mary Magdalene and that they had children. Jesus supported equality, relationships and the sacred feminine, but this support was not endorsed by the Church.

The Church was very much against treating women as equals. Constantine and his male successors successfully created a patriarchal Christianity. They waged war against the sacred feminine and effectively wiped out the sacred goddess from modern religions. The Church's protocol was set: it was to be run by men and priests were not to be married. In fact the whole idea of relationships, and even sex, became taboo.

The Witches' Hammer was published during the Catholic Inquisition. It warned about the dangers of "free thinking women," and was a used as a guide on how to identify torture and destroy them. The Church searched out women in power, including female scholars, mystics and midwives and killed them for their heretical practices. Heretical practices were those deemed by the Church not to be in line with its official position. According to the Church, death was God's rightful punishment for Eve's biting into the apple of knowledge, the original sin. Over a period of 300 years, more than five million women were burned at the stake by witch hunters.

Questions

o   If Rule #2 is *Freedom of Choice*, how does the choice to eat an apple become a sin?

o   Who really is proclaiming that this was the original sin of man? Was it God or was it man?

o   What if five million women died over a Church policy created by man, not God, proclaimed to be God's will? Did they die under false pretenses?

o   What kind of damage has this done to the spirit of the sacred feminine? How does this affect us today? Is this the basis for why women are devalued in our society?

o   If the relationship between Jesus and Mary Magdalene had been supported by the Church, what impact would that have had on our society today?

   o What impact would it have on our relationships today?

   o Would women have been treated the way they have been over the last 2,000 years?

   o What impact would that have on the patriarchal structure of the Church?

o What consequences have we endured because of this suppression on relationships and taboo on sex?

o If Catholic priests had been allowed to marry or if women had been allowed to be priests, would we have as many child molestation cases as we do today?

For every action there is a reaction. For every choice there are consequences.

Multiple Versions of the New Testament

While the religions were being combined, many of the gospels were rewritten or discarded altogether if they did not fit in with the official line of Christianity. The original conflicting gospels of Matthew, Mark, Luke and John were translated and rewritten according to the fashion and political whims of the day. There are about 5,000 manuscript versions of the New Testament in existence today and none of them are from earlier than the fourth century.

Non-Conforming Books

Many non-conforming books came out of this period that did not fit with the official Church line. They were in danger of being destroyed because of their heretical nature so they were hidden in Nag Hammadi, Egypt and were not discovered until December 1945. The books, called the Coptic Scrolls, date back to AD 400.

Most people are not aware that a number of books were written during this time, but were never included in the Bible. Here are a few of the titles:

Gospel of Thomas
Gospel of Philip
Apcryphon (The Secret Book of) John
Gospel of Truth

*Gospel of Egyptians (The Secret Book of the Great
    Invisible Spirit)*
Secret Book of James
Apocalypse of Paul
The Letter of Peter to Philip
The Apocalypse of Peter
Gospel of Mary Magdalene

What is it about these writings that kept them out of the Bible? Scholars say that at the time it was being compiled, Christians were confronted with a large variety of literature among which choices had to be made. Many of the books were discarded because they were written by lesser known authors, but many were discarded because they did not support the image of Jesus that they wanted to portray.

Refer back to Rule # 2, *Freedom of Choice*. The question is who was making the choices and what criteria were they using to decide? Would you make the same choices today?

The Gospel of Philip

The *Gospel of Philip*, for example, tells of a rivalry between Mary Magdalene and other male disciples.

…the companion to the savior is Mary Magdalene. Christ loves her more than all the disciples and used to kiss her on the mouth. The rest of the disciples were offended by it. They ask Jesus, "why do you love her more than all of us?"

Many of these gospels are referred to as the Gnostic Gospels. Gnostic literally means knowledge. The Gnostics believe that to know oneself is to know God. This is quite different from Orthodox Jews and Christians who believe that there is a gap that separates humanity from its creator. The Gnostics believe there is no gap between the Self and the Divine; they are one in the same.

The Jesus described in these gospels is a Jesus who talks about illusion and enlightenment, not of sin and repentance. Instead of coming to save us from our sins, he comes as a guide to spiritual understanding. A spiritual master. When disciples attain enlightenment, they are now equal with God.

The Gnostics rejected the Christian view of the resurrection. They insisted the resurrection was not a unique event in the past, but a symbol of how Christ's presence could be experienced in the present. What mattered was not the literal seeing, but the spiritual vision.

The *Gospel of Mary* describes the resurrection as appearance or visions received in dreams or ecstatic trances.

The *Apocalypse of Peter* tells how Peter, deep in trance saw Christ who explained that Christ is the intellectual spirit, filled with radiant light.

The *Gospel of Philip* also says that the resurrection can happen to you when you are alive, not dead. It refers to spiritual enlightenment.

The Gnostic gospels discuss how after Christ died, he appeared to his disciples in spiritual form, not literal form.

Now you can begin to see the problems facing the Church. How could they rule the masses if there were books around that said anybody could be God like? How could the men rule the Church if Jesus was portrayed of loving a women more than any other disciple? How could Jesus be a deity if he did not die for our sins and literally rise from the dead.

Therefore, the Apostle's Creed was written:

Christians confess that God is perfectly good, and still he created a world that includes pain, injustice and death: The Jesus of Nazareth was borne of a virgin mother and the after being executed; he arose from his grave on the third day[1].

This formed the basis for Christian Doctrine. Anything outside of it was deemed heretical and was to be destroyed. They accepted no other Gospels but the four in the New Testament (Mathew, Mark, Luke and John), which serve as the canon (guideline) to measure all future doctrine and practice.

Christians (Catholics, Protestants, and Orthodox) must:

1. Accept the canon of the New Testament
2. Confess the Apostle's Creed
3. Affirm specific forms of Church institutions

Gnostics believe you can make direct contact with God, but this did not fit within the institutional framework. Orthodox Christians believed that all authority was handed down from the apostles to bishops, priests and deacons. If you did not go through the Church, you could not be saved.

It is clear which group won the campaign, but at what cost? Over time, they have created an authoritative document (the Bible) that is incomplete at best. At worst, it's inaccurate.

Mixed Messages

There are many mixed messages in today's version of the Bible. Some stories carry the message that God is a loving God, yet go on to say that if you do not serve God you will not be saved. Which is it? Is God a loving God, or one that demands your total subservience? If God is a loving God, why would she punish you for making a mistake? If we truly have freedom of choice, why would God punish us for making a choice that is not "right" in God's eyes? If you do not accept Jesus as your savior, is it true that you will not be saved? What about all the

---

[1] Elaine Pagels, *The Gnostic Gospels*, 1979 Vintage

wonderful people in the world who practice Judaism, Buddhism, Hinduism, Islam or even nonreligious people? Are they all bad people because they will not be saved?

Understanding how the Bible came about, how it was actually put together starts to shed some light on why there are mixed messages. The message that God is a loving God is true, but the Church was fearful about controlling the masses so they chose fear and intimidation, just the like Romans. There is a reason it is called the Roman Catholic Church. The Church made rules to ensure structure and obedience. If you don't obey them you will burn in eternal damnation—pretty motivating stuff. The problem is that history is what the winners decide they want future generations to know. If you continually spin facts and pass down misinformation, you eventually forget what really happened and you begin to believe your own lies.

Finding the Truth

So how do you separate truth from bias? It is an act of discernment. If it is loving, caring and considerate of other people, it flows from truth. If it is manipulative, plays on fear and puts people, genders, races or other religions down, than it flows from bias. Follow your feelings and your heart.

We are all God's children, every one of us. We can all become one with God, whether we choose to do it through a church or not. We as a society have been making decisions based on an historical document that is inaccurate and incomplete. There is no doubt that we have experienced the consequences of these choices. Just look around and see for yourself. We still do not treat women and men equally. We still do not treat one race equal to another. We still choose to go to war with both sides thinking that God is behind them. Maybe God doesn't take sides. Maybe God doesn't like to see her children fighting at all.

Are we going to continue down this path or is it time to change? If we do not like where we are as a society, then we, as a society can choose differently.

Maybe it is time to reevaluate. Maybe it is time to choose differently...

RULE #5
The Trinity

In this world most everything can be broken down into three parts:

We are a three part being: Mind, Body, Soul

Religion:	Father, Son, Spirit
Psychologists:	Id, Ego, Superego Or Conscious, Subconscious, Super-conscious
Scientist:	Energy, Matter, Anti-matter
Time:	Past, Present, Future
Poets:	Mind, Heart, Soul
Space:	Here, There, Space in Between

When you engage *Freedom of Choice* and *Laws of the Universe*, you are creating energy on three different levels. You are making choices that affect the way you think, the way you feel and that invisible part of you called your soul.

This is important to understand because even though you know what is going on in your mind and your body, you may not be fully aware of what is going on in your soul.

Your soul never forgets what goals you had established for this life. That is why it is important for you to have quiet moments with yourself so you can reconnect with *you*. Look within yourself to see what you want to get out of your life. If you don't go *within*, you will go *without*.

Zero Point Field

Before Einstein died, one of the mysteries in life that interested him most was a little thing called the *zero point field*. All things in life are made of matter, but when you break everything down to the atomic level, whether you are talking about a pencil or a blade of grass, they all have the protons, neutrons and electrons. They also have the zero point field in common, which is the space between.

Einstein's theory was that pure energy from the zero point field allows all things to be connected. Maybe the famous line in the movie Star Wars, "May the force be with you" was not that far off.

It is this field of energy that connects us to the energy of the universe and allows the *Laws of the Universe* to work.

You were energy before you were born and you become energy when you die, and while you are on earth every thought you have, every word you speak and every action you take sends ripples into this field of energy. The good news is that you have control over your life (whether you realize it or not). If you are consistently sending out good vibes into the universe, the universe will keep on sending them back to you. The bad news is the system works just as efficiently if you are sending bad vibes into the universe as well.

RULE #6
Relativity

Black or White
Right or Wrong
Light and Dark
Good and Bad

You can't have one thing without the other. You cannot feel love if there is no sorrow. You cannot feel joy if there is no sadness. You would not understand light if there wasn't darkness. You cannot have good without the bad. You cannot have matter without the anti-matter.

Many people think that God should make all of the pain in the world go away. No more hunger. No more disease. No more pain. These, unfortunately, are an essential part of the entire whole. You cannot understand the pleasure and comfort of being full from eating a delicious meal if you have never felt hunger. You can't understand the concept of feeling healthy if you have never experienced the agony of being sick. You cannot understand how wonderful it is to feel normal if you have never felt pain. There can't be heaven if there's no hell.

Relativity is a key component of *The Rule(s) of Our Game*. It's what makes the rule of *Freedom of Choice* so tough. All choices have consequences that can be either good or bad, but it is the fear of experiencing bad consequences that help shape your choices. God will not punish you for a poor choice, but you may not like the consequences because of the rule of *Relativity*.

For example, if you really enjoyed going out and drinking with your friends, you may hesitate to drink too much if you know that you will have a horrible hangover the next day. Your fear of the pending hangover may affect your choices for the evening.

This assumes the ability to have good judgment and make good decisions. Our society has done a very poor job acknowledging up front that when alcohol is consumed or drugs are used, judgment is one of the first casualties. Poor choices are made like driving while impaired, which so many times leads to tragic consequences.

If you choose to drink, make a plan that includes a designated driver when you are sober and still have the ability to make good choices.

Hell is Not What You Think

As mentioned before, there can't be heaven if there is no hell. The reality is that there is no hell as society has portrayed it. There is no fire or brimstone. There are no pitchforks. Hell is the opposite of joy. It is knowing your potential and not reaching it. It is being away from God in a very dark place. There are people who are experiencing their own version of hell right now. Sadly, they arrived there through a series of their own choices. Hopefully they will realize that they don't have to stay there and they will start to find their way back to the light. Back to love.

There are so many people on earth who are experiencing hell. They do not feel love. They do not have hope. They are miserable. They are out of the light. They are in the dark. This is true hell. If you find yourself in this situation use *The Rule(s) of our Game(s)* to change your circumstances. Climb out of that deep dark hole one step at a time and walk toward the light.

If you know of someone who is in this despair, throw them a life line. Share *The Rule(s) of Our Game(s)* with them so they will have the tools to change their circumstances.

There is no reason for people to continue to experience hell unless it is of their own choosing.

RULE #7
Fear and Love

All human emotions stem from either fear or love. You may be living your life in constant fear and not even know it. Are you quick to criticize others? Do you always come from a place of scarcity, constantly worrying about not having enough—enough food, enough money, enough friends? Or are you living a life of love? Are you quick to praise others? Do you come from a place of abundance? Do you always seem to have enough of everything?

Hatred is obviously a fear-based emotion. Do you allow room in your heart for hatred? It is true that without the emotion of hatred we would not fully understand love, but that does not mean that we have to allocate time to it.

There are so many people in the world who pass on hate. They pass it on to their children, to their neighbors and friends. Hate is such a negative emotion and no good can come from it. People criticize people from other races, people from different countries, and people from different religions. They do this because they feel superior by putting them down.

The reality is critical people are afraid of other people because they are different. They look different, they come from different backgrounds, or they have different beliefs. They have convinced themselves that they are superior to other people, but they are wrong. We are all equal in the eyes of God. We are all God's children. It doesn't matter what color your skin is, where you live, or what you believe in. You are not better that anyone else. Treat all others equally.

Where do You Dwell?

Take some time to reevaluate how you treat and view other people. There are many variations of fear. It has an enormous impact on decisions and quality of life. Fear is negative energy. If you are constantly sending out negative energy into the universe, there's no question what will come back to you. It is a self-fulfilling prophecy. For instance, the minute you love someone, your next thought will be one of fear. You'll be afraid that you will not be loved back. If you are going to love someone, love them unconditionally like God loves you.

As you make your way through life, make conscious choices about where your emotions are rooted. Choose praise. Choose abundance. Choose love. Love unconditionally and the world will be a better place.

You have heard it time and time again: "All you need is love…Love is all you need." Another way to put it is "You don't need fear…You don't need hatred." Throw away all fear-based emotions and replace them with love-based emotions.

If we are all going to die when our lives are over and go back to where we came from, there is no need to be petty toward our neighbors while we all share this planet. It is a waste of time and energy.

Christianity's Biggest Flaw

Christianity is a fear-based religion. That's its major flaw. Fearing God is what is taught. Accept Jesus as your only savior or you will not be saved.

Fear and intimidation was used in the Bible as a way of crowd control. It was the way the Church chose to control the masses. Strike the *fear* of God in them and they will stay behaved. That will guarantee that they will have to go through the Church if they want to be saved.

The truth is that God loves all of us. We are all God's children, just like Jesus was. Jesus spent time on this earth giving us lessons on how to treat one another with respect. God sent Jesus to us to save us from ourselves. That doesn't mean that now you have to accept Jesus as your savior or be left out. There are many of God's children on this earth who believe in a higher being and do not believe that Jesus was a God. This does not mean that they are wrong and Christians are right.

Another problem with Christians and Christianity is they believe they are superior to anyone who believes differently. They believe that they have it right and everyone else has it wrong. We are all created equal and this feeling of superiority leads to no good. It is harmful and destructive. It creates mistrust and leads to fear and hatred and is completely unnecessary.

Jesus did amazing things during his brief life on this planet, but look deeply at the message that he repeated over and over: "Love thy neighbor." All you need is love. Treat others with respect. Be a good citizen of earth.

This difference between the Christian religion and other religions will continue to cause our society grief and drive a chasm between good people. If you are Christian and you choose to place more emphasis on Jesus that is fine. But do not judge other people who choose not to. Do not make the mistake of thinking that you are a more righteous person because you have accepted Jesus as your savior. This will alienate others who believe differently. Just because their beliefs are different, doesn't make them wrong. We are all equal in the eyes of God.

RULE #8
The Language of God

Many people want to talk to God but they don't know how. They have all these images of how God talks to people from the Bible and from modern movies, but they do not know how it works in real life.

To have a conversation with God, you need to know that the Language of God is through feelings. Feelings are how God talks to you everyday and feelings are how you can start talking back. Remember, we are a part of a trinity: mind, body and soul. It is through the soul and feelings that you can make a connection with God. Generally speaking, women seem to be more in touch with their feelings so they seem to have an advantage over most men in this area. It's called "women's intuition" when they have a feeling they should do one thing or another.

Again, this is why having quiet time with yourself is so vitally important. How can you carry on a conversation with God if you cannot hear her? No one can carry on a conversation in all the noise of life—the TV blaring, the kids screaming, the dog barking.

Find a quiet place just to "be" from time to time. We are after all human BEings, not human DOings. Express your thoughts to God and listen for her reply. Some people call this prayer. Call it anything you want because labeling it is not important. Doing it is. This is where you can get re-acquainted with what your life goals truly are. Have you drifted away from those goals? It is so easy to do.

Now that you know about the energy in the zero point field and the connectivity between your mind, body and soul, it is not too far of a stretch to know that you can communicate with God over this beam of energy.

If you have never talked to God, now would be a great time to start.

Communication from God

If your feeling is based in love, more likely than not it is communication from God. If it is fear-based, it is coming from you. If your feelings warn you of danger, pay attention. If your feelings are telling you to harm someone, then those feelings need to be evaluated because they are not coming from God.

You do not need to learn a new language to talk to God, you only need to pay closer attention.

RULE #1
The Golden Rule

As you have probably figured out by now, Rule #1 is *The Golden Rule*. Do to others as you would like done to you. Now that you know how the universe works, another way to look at it is: Others will do to you what you do to them.

This is the main message from Jesus and the first rule. We get so caught up in our daily lives and our micro drama's that we forget it too easily. The outcome of life is not in question. The question is what you will have done with your time while you were here and how did you treat others.

If this is the only rule you follow, the world be a better place. Unfortunately this rule is broken the most. Many times we do not treat others how we want to be treated.

All You Need is Love

This is what it is all about. All you need is love. It has been around forever. We have heard it, but we really didn't understand what it meant until now.

There is a rhythm to how we treat our heroes. At first we love them and build them up. We make them heroes. Then we love to tear them down and destroy them. Then we love them again. This is a viscous cycle that is played out time and time again in our society. Perhaps we could choose to eliminate steps two and three. Love them. Make them your heroes, but if they make poor choices, do not judge them or tear them down. Love them unconditionally and they will do the same to you.

J.W. Goethe

I have come to the frightening conclusion that I am the decisive element.

It is my personal approach that creates the climate.

It is my daily mood that makes the weather.

I possess tremendous power to make life miserable or joyous.
I can be a tool of torture or an instrument of inspiration;
I can humiliate or humor, hurt or heal.

In all situations,
it is my response that decides whether
a crisis is escalated or de-escalated, and a person is humanized or de-humanized.
If we treat people as they are,
we make them worse.
If we treat people as they ought to be,
we help them become what they are capable of becoming.

Conclusion

So there you have it: *The Rule(s) of Our Game(s)*. If you start playing by these rules, your life will become better. If we as a society begin playing by these rules, our world will become a better place.

Imagine a world where everyone was treated equally and with respect. Imagine a world with lower crime rates and fewer wars. Imagine a world with no hunger or starvation. Imagine a world with more love in it.

If you can imagine it, you can make it happen ... and now you know how!

ACKNOWLEDGMENTS

I want to thank Mary Myers of Myers Communications, without whom I am sure I would not be in possession of a final product! Thank you so much for your patience, help and support through the process of editing this book. Thank you to Kent Hermes from Thought Dog Consulting, LLC for setting up the social media network and Susan Straub-Martin from Strauberry Studios for the graphic designs. Thank you to Celeste from Bennett & Hastings Publishing for help with the final touches. Finally, I want to thank all of my friends, family and co-workers who were so helpful and supportive along the way ... there are pieces of all of you woven throughout the pages of this book.